What Was the Battle of Gettysburg?

What Was the Battle of Gettysburg?

by Jim O'Connor

illustrated by John Mantha

Grosset & Dunlap

An Imprint of Penguin Group (USA) Inc.

In memory of Private Charles Spiesberger,
killed in action on Little Round Top,
July 2, 1863—JOC

GROSSET & DUNLAP
Published by the Penguin Group
Penguin Group (USA) Inc., 375 Hudson Street, New York, New York 10014, USA
Penguin Group (Canada), 90 Eglinton Avenue East, Suite 700,
Toronto, Ontario M4P 2Y3, Canada
(a division of Pearson Penguin Canada Inc.)
Penguin Books Ltd, 80 Strand, London WC2R 0RL, England
Penguin Ireland, 25 St Stephen's Green, Dublin 2, Ireland
(a division of Penguin Books Ltd)
Penguin Group (Australia), 707 Collins Street, Melbourne, Victoria 3008, Australia
(a division of Pearson Australia Group Pty Ltd)
Penguin Books India Pvt Ltd, 11 Community Centre,
Panchsheel Park, New Delhi—110 017, India
Penguin Group (NZ), 67 Apollo Drive, Rosedale, Auckland 0632, New Zealand
(a division of Pearson New Zealand Ltd)
Penguin Books (South Africa), Rosebank Office Park, 181 Jan Smuts Avenue,
Parktown North 2193, South Africa
Penguin China, B7 Jiaming Center, 27 East Third Ring Road North,
Chaoyang District, Beijing 100020, China

Penguin Books Ltd, Registered Offices: 80 Strand, London WC2R 0RL, England

Text copyright © 2013 by Jim O'Connor. Cover and interior illustrations copyright
© 2013 by Penguin Group (USA) Inc. All rights reserved. Published by Grosset & Dunlap,
a division of Penguin Young Readers Group, 345 Hudson Street, New York, New York
10014. GROSSET & DUNLAP is a trademark of Penguin Group (USA) Inc.
Printed in the U.S.A.

Library of Congress Control Number: 2012027557

ISBN 978-0-448-46286-8 (pbk)   10 9 8 7 6 5 4 3 2 1
ISBN 978-0-448-46575-3 (hc)   10 9 8 7 6 5 4 3 2 1

Contents

What Was the Battle of Gettysburg?. 1

A Small Town in Pennsylvania 12

On the Lookout. .22

Day One: July 1, 1863. 26

Day Two: July 2, 1863 42

Day Three: July 3, 1863. 55

Day Three: Pickett's Charge 63

The Day After: July 4, 1863. 82

The Gettysburg Address. 90

A Soldier's Letter Home 100

Timelines. 104

Bibliography. .106

What Was the Battle of Gettysburg?

Today, many Americans think the Civil War, or the "War between the States," was just about slavery. Twenty-five states in the North fought to end slavery, while eleven states in the South fought just as hard to keep the right to own slaves.

Slavery was certainly the biggest issue of the war. But there were other reasons for the Civil War.

One issue was states' rights. That meant how much power each state had over itself. What if states no longer wanted to be part of the United States of America? Did they have the right to break away and start their own country? The South said, "Yes, we can do that if we want." The North said, "No, we're one country, and that is the way it has to stay."

In the years before the war began, many Southern states felt that the antislavery North was threatening their way of life. Cotton was the

main industry throughout most of the South. Cotton was grown on farms called plantations. Some plantations were huge. Somerset Place in North Carolina had more than 100,000 acres of land.

Southern cotton growers used slaves as unpaid workers. Large plantations required many slaves to plant, weed, and pick the crops. It was not uncommon for rich cotton growers,

called "Cotton Kings," to own five hundred slaves.

Slaves belonged to their owners in the same way that horses and cows did. Slaves had no rights. They could not vote. They could not own property. They were sold at auctions. By 1860 there were almost four million slaves living in the South.

In the North, the land was not suitable for growing cotton or tobacco, another big crop in the South. Northern farms were small. More and more people worked in factories and businesses. Although in the early days of the United States some people in the Northern states had owned slaves, slavery had largely died out. By the 1820s, many people in the North thought slavery was horribly wrong. It had to be abolished—or ended—everywhere in the United States.

The Abolitionist Movement grew stronger in the years before the Civil War. A novel called *Uncle Tom's Cabin*, by Harriet Beecher Stowe, came out in 1852. It dramatized the harsh life of slaves and sold an amazing 300,000 copies in one year. It won the abolitionists many new followers.

There had always been tension between the North and South. But it was growing much worse.

When Abraham Lincoln was elected president in 1860, it was the last straw for the Southern states. Lincoln was against slavery and did not want it spreading to any new state that came into the Union. He also believed that states did not have the right to secede, or leave, the Union.

Union flag

But that is just what seven Southern states did in early 1861. They formed the Confederate States of America. Later, four more states also seceded.

On April 12, 1861, Confederate gunners

Confederate flag

opened fire on Fort Sumter in Charleston Harbor, South Carolina. The bombardment lasted thirty-four hours and left the fort a pile of rubble. Amazingly, there were no Union casualties. Fort Sumter soon surrendered. The Civil War had begun.

Fort Sumter

MINNESOTA

WISCONSIN

MICHIGAN

IOWA

ILLINOIS

INDIANA

OHIO

MISSOURI

KENTUCKY

ARKANSAS

TENNESSEE

MISSISSIPPI

ALABAMA

GEORGIA

LOUISIANA

FLORIDA

MAINE

N. HAMPSHIRE

VERMONT

NEW YORK

MASSACHUSETTS

RHODE ISLAND

CONNECTICUT

PENNSYLVANIA

NEW JERSEY

DELAWARE

WASHINGTON, DC

MARYLAND

VIRGINIA

N. CAROLINA

S. CAROLINA

Atlantic Ocean

1861

Union States ▨

Confederate States ☐

Jefferson Davis

Jefferson Davis was the first and only president of the Confederate States of America. He was born in Kentucky on June 3, 1808, only about one hundred miles from where Abraham Lincoln was born on February 12, 1809.

Davis graduated from West Point. That is the United States Military Academy in West Point, New York. Many famous soldiers as well as US presidents have graduated from West Point. Davis served in the United States Army and later became a rich cotton grower in Mississippi. Like all cotton growers, Davis owned slaves. He had at least seventy-four slaves working on his plantation. One named William Jackson worked in Davis's house and later became a spy for the Union during the war.

Davis served two terms as United States senator from Mississippi. Oddly, before the Civil War started, Davis argued in Congress against Southern states breaking away from the Union. He wanted Southern states to find a way for Congress to let them keep their slaves. However, in 1861, after seven Southern states left the Union, Jefferson Davis resigned his seat in the Senate.

In November 1861, he was elected president of the Confederate States. His vice president was Alexander H. Stephens from Georgia. He had served in the US House of Representatives.

Jefferson Davis was a cold and demanding leader. His best decision was appointing Robert E. Lee to command the Confederate troops.

When the war ended, Davis was arrested and charged with treason. However, there was never a trial. Jefferson Davis was released from prison in 1867 and died in New Orleans on December 6, 1889.

CHAPTER 1
A Small Town in Pennsylvania

In July 1863, two massive armies fought a deadly battle around the little town of Gettysburg, Pennsylvania.

The American Civil War had been raging for two years, North against South. A civil war is when

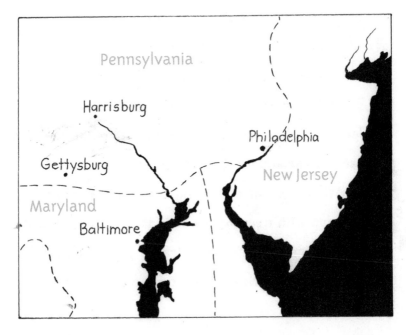

people of the same country go to war against one another. Brothers fight brothers, fathers oppose sons, long friendships end in hatred and death.

Union soldier   **Confederate soldier**

Gettysburg was not the first battle of the Civil War. And it was not the last. But it was the bloodiest. About one hundred and sixty-five thousand soldiers took part in it, ninety thousand Union soldiers against seventy-five thousand Southern soldiers. When the battle ended after three days, a total of about fifty thousand men were dead, wounded, or missing. After Gettysburg, the Civil War would go on for two more years. Fighting didn't stop until the South surrendered on April 9, 1865.

Robert E. Lee surrenders to Ulysses S. Grant

Gettysburg is still considered the most famous battle of the war. Why? At Gettysburg, the tide turned. Up until then, the South had been winning. After Gettysburg, the Confederates were no longer sure their army was unbeatable. And after two years of losing battles, the Northern forces gained pride and confidence. They believed the war was theirs to win. And they were right.

Gettysburg was a prosperous market town of 2,400 people. A network of ten roads extended out from town like the spokes of a wheel. Until July 1863, Gettysburg was not well known like other cities in Pennsylvania such as Philadelphia or Harrisburg.

Neither side planned to fight at Gettysburg. Pennsylvania was a Northern state. So far, battles had been fought all over the South, in Tennessee, Louisiana, Virginia, North Carolina, South Carolina, Maryland, Kentucky, Mississippi, West Virginia, Texas, and Georgia. The farthest north that any fighting had taken place was around Washington, DC.

Confederate States

But now Confederate General Robert E. Lee had a new idea. Lee was the top general of the Southern army. He wanted to whip the Northern army on their own land. So he sent his troops north into the lush farmlands of Pennsylvania. First they could get supplies. They would go into stores and onto farms, forcing people to sell them whatever they needed—food, shoes, clothes.

The Southern soldiers paid in Confederate money that was worthless in the North.

By starting a battle in Pennsylvania, Lee would lure away some Northern troops fighting in the South. The Northern army remaining in the South would be smaller, less powerful. That increased the rebels' chances of winning more and more victories.

In Pennsylvania, Lee wanted to pick the best places for his men to fight from. For instance, the tops of hills. From there, soldiers could see down in all directions and destroy an oncoming army. Once Lee had entrenched his troops in the Pennsylvania hills, he hoped they'd wipe out the Northern forces.

Lee hoped that if his plan worked, the Union

would have to surrender. The war would end for good. Abraham Lincoln would have to recognize the Confederacy as a separate country.

General Lee's plan got off to a promising start. He moved his army into Pennsylvania with little trouble. By June 29, his troops were preparing to attack Harrisburg, the state capital.

Robert E. Lee

General Robert Edward Lee was born on January 19, 1807, at Stratford Hall Plantation in Virginia. His father, Henry "Light-Horse Harry" Lee, had been a hero in the Revolutionary War.

Lee graduated second in his class at West Point. During the Mexican-American War, he served for a time with Ulysses S. Grant. Grant was the general Lee would surrender to in 1865, ending the Civil War.

Lee thought that the Southern states were wrong to secede. He also called slavery "a moral and political evil in any country."

When the war started, President Lincoln asked Lee to become the commander of the Union Army.

Lee said no. He had decided to join the Confederacy.

Why?

Robert E. Lee felt very loyal to his home state of Virginia. The Lees were one of Virginia's oldest families. His wife was a great-granddaughter of Martha Custis, who married George Washington.

When Jefferson Davis asked him to lead the Southern troops, Lee accepted. He was a smart general whose troops were devoted to him. But he was soundly beaten at Gettysburg. It was the turning point of the Civil War.

After the war, Lee became president of Washington College in Virginia. (It was renamed Washington and Lee after his death.) Robert E. Lee died on October 12, 1870, in Lexington, Virginia.

CHAPTER 2
On the Lookout

The Northern army knew Lee was in Pennsylvania. But where?

On June 30, Union cavalry scouted ahead of the larger army that was moving slowly north from Virginia. The scouts rode into Gettysburg. There they heard that a large Confederate army

was north and west of town. They reported to their commander, General John Buford.

Buford thought that Gettysburg was a good place to stop the Confederate advance through

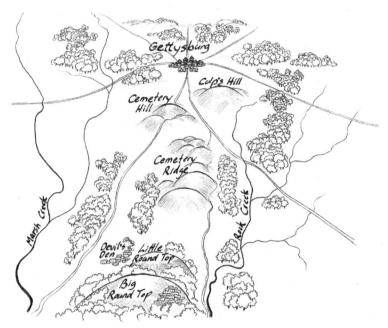

Pennsylvania. A series of ridges west of the town would give his men good cover. Buford didn't have nearly enough men to defeat the greater Southern forces. But his soldiers could keep the Confederates at bay until more Union troops

arrived. Buford told one of his officers, "They will attack you in the morning and will come booming, skirmishers three deep. You will have to fight like the devil to hold your own."

General Buford

Buford sent a messenger to his commander, Major General John Reynolds. Buford said he expected to be attacked the next day. It was urgent that more troops arrive quickly.

As night fell, General Buford posted soldiers along all the roads leading into Gettysburg from the east, west, and north. The troops stationed to the west of town were spread out along one of the ridges. They were told to let Buford know as soon as they spotted rebel troops.

Even with a bigger army, the Northern soldiers would have a tough time beating the rebels. The Union troops had suffered a string of losses.

Lee had proved himself a better leader than the Northern generals.

General Buford needed a good lookout post. The nearby Lutheran Seminary had a cupola, a small tower, on its roof. From there, Buford could see in all directions. Once the sun rose, he would spot the enemy coming. He also hoped that he would see General Reynolds and his men marching from the south to help out.

Until then, all he could do was wait.

CHAPTER 3
Day One: July 1, 1863

Around seven thirty the next morning, two brigades of Confederate soldiers were marching toward Gettysburg. Their leader was General Henry Heth.

The day before, Heth's scouts had reported seeing Union cavalry near Gettysburg. He figured it was a small group of local soldiers. His men could handle them easily.

General Heth

He should have sent out patrols to find out exactly how many Northern soldiers were nearby. But he didn't. This was a big mistake.

Union soldiers along the ridge saw a cloud of

dust coming toward them. It was the rebel forces. When the enemy troops drew closer, a young Union officer named Marcellus Jones borrowed a type of gun called a carbine from one of his men. He laid it across the top rail of a fence, took careful aim, and fired. It was the first shot in the bloody battle of Gettysburg.

Infantry (soldiers on foot) on both sides carried guns called muskets. A soldier had to stand to reload his five-foot-long musket. This took time and exposed him to enemy fire.

The Union cavalry, however, was outfitted with a new kind of rifle called a Sharps Carbine. These rifles were small, only thirty-nine inches long. Soldiers could easily reload them while they were sitting or lying down. They simply slid a cartridge into a slot on the side of the carbine. This let Union soldiers fire about six rounds a minute, which was twice as fast as the muskets

could fire. Also, the soldiers with carbines could stay hidden from the enemy while reloading their guns.

Although the rebels outnumbered them, Union soldiers did exactly what General Buford wanted. They slowed down the Confederate advance.

As the rebels brought more troops forward, Buford's men had to retreat half a mile to another ridge. The rebels surged forward, thinking they had the enemy on the run.

Then at the next ridge, the rebels were caught off guard. Two more Union cavalry brigades were waiting. Six cannons blocked the road. The increased **Sharps carbine** firepower drove the rebels back. But not for long. Within an hour, they were on the attack with several thousand more men.

At about ten thirty, Union General John Reynolds arrived with some aides at Gettysburg. They galloped to the Lutheran Seminary building, where Reynolds found Buford. "What's the matter, John?" Reynolds asked.

"There's the devil to pay," Buford answered. He

quickly filled Reynolds in. His troops had succeeded in slowing down the enemy infantry. But they couldn't hold out much longer.

So Reynolds sent a messenger to his army a few miles away. "Get

General Meade

to Gettysburg quickly. There is no time to waste."

Reynolds sent another messenger to General George G. Meade's headquarters in Taneytown, Maryland. An army of eighty thousand was there. Meade was general in chief of the entire Union Army. Meade was told about the large rebel forces at Gettysburg. However, Reynolds refused to give up, the messenger reported. Reynolds would resist the rebels "inch by inch." This was the place to fight Lee. Reynolds needed Meade's large army to do that.

Reynolds's first two brigades came onto the

battlefield at about ten thirty in the morning. One of the brigades was the famous "Iron Brigade" from Wisconsin, Indiana, and Michigan. The Iron Brigade wore distinctive black stovepipe hats. The rebels had fought them before and knew that the Iron Brigade was tough, brave, and never backed down.

Reynolds was directing the action. "Forward, men, forward for God's sake." Suddenly, he fell from his horse to the ground. He had been shot in the head.

"I never saw a man die more quickly," a soldier reported.

This was a huge loss for the Union. Reynolds

was one of their most experienced officers. He was also very good at planning battles. Now he was gone.

Reynolds's men laid his body under a nearby tree. Today, visitors to Gettysburg can see a monument marking the spot where the general fell.

Reynolds was the highest-ranking officer on either side to die at Gettysburg. His replacement was General Abner Doubleday. In 1861, Doubleday had been stationed at Fort Sumter where the Civil War started. (Later, after the war was over, Doubleday would be credited with inventing the game of baseball, but this is not so.)

Doubleday's job was to hold the rebels back as long as he could. It would take several hours for Meade and his men to reach Gettysburg. The Iron Brigade lived up to its reputation. They swept throughout the woods and pushed the rebels back up the Chambersburg Pike.

They also captured Confederate General James Archer. Doubleday and Archer knew each other from before the war.

"Good morning, Archer," Doubleday said as the Southern general was brought before him. "How are you? I'm glad to see you."

Archer refused to shake hands with his old

friend. "Well, I'm not glad to see you," he replied.

Meanwhile, the battle was changing minute by minute. Doubleday saw that the right side of the Union line had begun to retreat toward town. The rebels, under the command of General Joseph Davis, were moving so quickly that they ran right past Doubleday and his men.

Doubleday immediately sent a regiment after them. The Confederates, now under attack from both sides, looked for a way to escape. They found an unused railroad "cut," or trench. It seemed to offer good cover. The rebels scrambled into it only to discover that the steep sides were too deep to shoot over.

Union troops blocked both ends of the trench and set up a deadly crossfire. Dozens of rebels were killed in only a few minutes. Davis's men had no choice but to surrender.

The Union would not be able to enjoy this small victory for very long. More and more Confederate troops were joining the battle from the north and west. In fact, almost the whole rebel army was about to descend on Gettysburg. Doubleday ordered his men to retreat through town and up onto Culp's Hill and Cemetery Ridge. This was about a mile away.

The fighting continued right on the streets of

Gettysburg, with many Union soldiers killed or captured. At the gatehouse of the town cemetery, a sign said, "All persons using firearms in these grounds will be prosecuted with the utmost rigor of the law." This sign had been put up long before the war came to Gettysburg. The words were ignored by soldiers on both sides for the next three days.

About half the Union troops made their way safely to the two hills. Their first task was to dig in and build temporary walls and trenches.

The rebels were close behind. If the Southerners had organized a charge up the hills right then, they could have overpowered Doubleday's men and captured the important high ground.

But a Confederate officer held his men back. This was a terrible mistake. Who knows? Had the right decision been made, the outcome of the Battle of Gettysburg might have been very different.

Rebel soldiers are surrounded in a trench.

July 1 ended with the Union troops on Culp's Hill and strung along Cemetery Ridge from Cemetery Hill to Little Round Top. They had suffered heavy losses. Almost ten thousand men had been killed or captured, but they kept the high ground.

The Southern forces were camped in Gettysburg and the surrounding fields. The rebels had lost about eight thousand men. They had also lost the high ground.

It had been a very bloody day. But worse was to come.

Mathew Brady

The Civil War was the first major war with a photographic record of the death and destruction caused by battles. In earlier wars, artists sketched scenes that later ran in newspapers and magazines.

Mathew Brady was the most well known of the Civil War photographers. Brady and his men did not photograph combat. Photo equipment was too large and heavy to carry into battles. They brought their whole darkroom along in the back of a horse-drawn wagon to develop pictures.

Sometimes, photographers would move bodies to create better pictures. A famous photograph from Gettysburg was staged to show a dead Confederate soldier with his musket propped against a boulder.

CHAPTER 4
Day Two: July 2, 1863

While Union troops tried to catch a few hours of sleep, General George G. Meade arrived at Gettysburg. It was one o'clock in the morning on July 2. His army of eighty thousand men was not far behind him and would arrive soon. Meade

Union General George Meade

Confederate General
Richard Ewell

Confederate General
James P. Longstreet

Confederate dead at Gettysburg

Devil's Den

Little Round Top

Gettysburg, 1863

Union dead at Gettysburg

Jefferson Davis, president
of the Confederate States
of America

Confederate General
George E. Pickett, who
led the disastrous charge

Tombstones in the cemetery at Gettysburg Military Park

Lincoln's Address at the Dedication of the Gettysburg National Cemetery, November 19, 1863.

Abraham Lincoln giving his famous address at Gettysburg

As president, Abraham Lincoln was commander in chief of the Union forces.

Joshua Chamberlain, a Union general awarded the Medal of Honor for his efforts at Gettysburg

Confederate General Jeb Stuart, Lee's trusted scout

General Robert E. Lee, the commanding officer of all Confederate forces

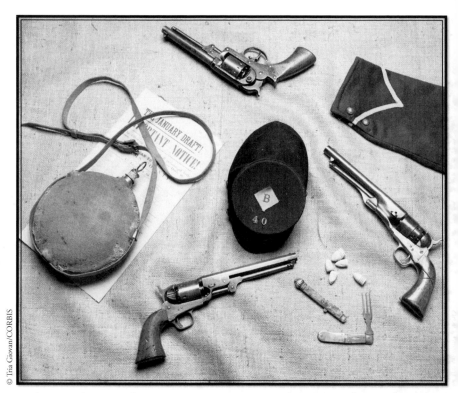

Union revolvers and gear

Union knapsack with artifacts, including a bayonet

Surgeon's coat and medical kit

Amputation kit dating back to 1863

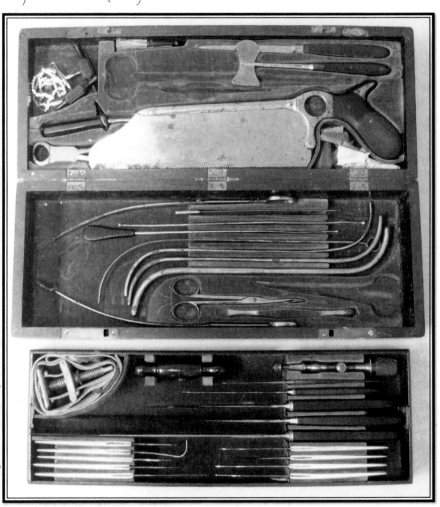

Union soldier from the 22nd New York State Militia at Harpers Ferry,
Virginia

Confederate soldiers standing next to the Model 1857 gun howitzer
("Napoleon"), the most common field artillery of the Civil War

7th New York State Militia officer in uniform

Portrait of Union soldiers from the Company I, 24th Infantry regiment, one of 175 regiments of African American soldiers who were first recruited in 1863

Two African American Union soldiers in full uniforms

African American Union soldier with his family

toured the area and discussed a battle plan with other officers.

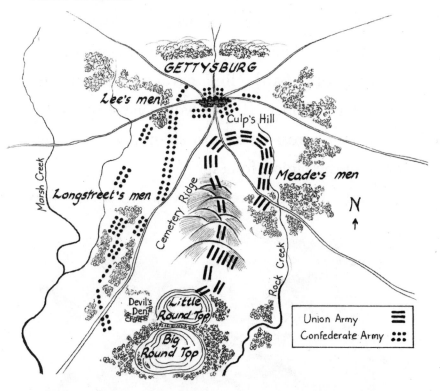

The troops were spread out over almost four miles. That is a very long battle line. But geography had worked in the Union's favor. One end of their line hooked back like a reverse fishhook. Culp's Hill and Little Round Top were only two miles apart. General Meade wanted his reinforcements to stay behind the ridge in between these two hills. That way he would be able to easily move men to wherever on the line they were most needed.

The long battle line gave Meade another advantage. Robert E. Lee would have to spread his troops across an almost six-mile-long line to contain the Union forces.

More brigades were arriving to strengthen

each army. Men slept by campfires that dotted the hills and fields around Gettysburg. Soldiers cleaned their equipment; many wrote letters to their families. Often they complained about the food, the weather, and boredom. They asked for socks, sewing kits, wool blankets, and more letters from home.

Long before dawn on July 2, Robert E. Lee of the South and George Meade of the North were both planning for the day's battle.

Meade's strategy was simple. He would place cannons along the entire line from Cemetery Hill to Little Round Top. Infantry would fill in between the cannons. The army was in place to bombard any part of the battlefield below.

Lee met with James Longstreet and Richard Ewell, two generals under his command, to discuss the plan for the day. The two younger officers disagreed about what to do. The day before, Ewell had hesitated about chasing after

Union troops. Now he wanted to attack the Union line between the two hills. He thought doing this would force General Meade to move troops from a third hill, Culp's Hill, in order to help out the Northern units under attack. Then Ewell's men could charge up Culp's Hill and take it. They would have a good spot from which to fire at the enemy.

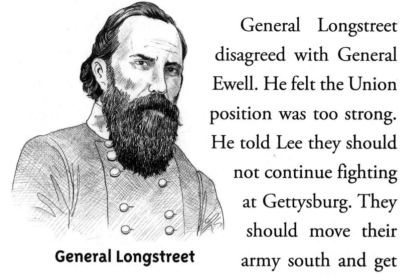

General Longstreet

General Longstreet disagreed with General Ewell. He felt the Union position was too strong. He told Lee they should not continue fighting at Gettysburg. They should move their army south and get between the Union army and Washington, DC. Meade would have to come after them. They could find a battlefield that would give them the advantage over the North.

Lee said, "We will stay in Gettysburg and finish them off." After all, the South had beaten Northern soldiers two times at Bull Run, and also at Fredericksburg and Chancellorsville. He believed his men could roll over anything. All along his idea had been to fight in Pennsylvania— and win!

Longstreet had no choice but to accept Lee and Ewell's plan. Now he argued in favor of the Confederate soldiers taking a route that would keep them hidden from the enemy. It was a longer route, but worth it in Longstreet's opinion. Lee agreed. Unfortunately, the troops did not get into place until the afternoon. This gave the Union side hours to dig in and prepare for an attack.

Union General Dan Sickles was in charge of anchoring the left end of the Union line at Little Round Top. Sickles had no military training. He'd been a state senator from New York before the war. All on his own, he decided to move his troops a half mile forward into an area known as Devil's Den. Other troops under Sickles were placed in a peach orchard and still others in a wheat field.

General Sickles

Sickles did all this without General Meade's permission. (Meade would not have given the okay for this.)

At four o'clock, the Confederates finally started their attack. They were surprised to find Sickles's men so far ahead of the rest of the Union line. In the fierce fighting that followed, Sickles's Union troops suffered heavy losses.

After the war, Sickles insisted that his plan was much better than Meade's. Sickles would even try to take credit for the Union victory. But most historians think what Sickles did was a mistake.

Sickles's men retreated. Those that were still alive wound up where Meade had originally placed them. As for Sickles, the war ended for him that afternoon when a cannonball shattered his right leg. He was carried from the battlefield to a first-aid station where the leg had to be cut off. Sickles did not want the army doctor to just throw his leg away, so he had an aide retrieve

the leg. After the war
Sickles put the bones in
a box shaped like a coffin.
He donated it to a museum
in Washington, DC. He visited his leg
every year on July 2, the anniversary of the battle.

Meanwhile, Little Round Top was totally
unprotected. Union General Gouverneur Warren

discovered the deserted summit and sent a frantic message to Meade: "Send troops now."

General Meade sent companies from Maine, New York, Pennsylvania, and Michigan to secure Little Round Top. They succeeded. And although Little Round Top was attacked again and again, it was never captured.

The Story of the 140th and Charlie Spiesberger

The New York 140th Infantry was among the companies fighting to control Little Round Top. It was from Rochester, New York, and was led by Colonel Patrick O'Rorke. The O'Rorkes were an immigrant Irish family. Many of the men in the New York 140th were immigrants like him. More than five hundred thousand soldiers who fought in the Civil War had not been born in the United States.

Eighteen-year-old Charlie Spiesberger was one of the young immigrant recruits in the 140th. (His family was from Austria.) He had only been in the army for nine months. The letters that he wrote home were in German. In one, he said that he hoped his parents would use money he had sent for themselves and to fix up the house.

He arrived at Gettysburg with the rest of the company in the early-morning hours of July 2. They had marched for hours. Some of the men walked barefoot because of the blisters on their feet.

O'Rorke and his men had to help hold Little Round Top. They reached the crest just as Confederate soldiers were coming up the other side. The rebels were only thirty feet away.

Immediately O'Rorke led a charge down the hill. Seconds later he was shot in the neck and killed. Charlie and the rest of the 140th continued the charge. The rebels were pushed back. Little Round Top was in Union hands.

Besides O'Rorke, twenty-five soldiers from the 140th died that afternoon. One of them was eighteen-year-old Charlie Spiesberger. He was my grandfather's uncle.

—Jim O'Connor

Confederate General Ewell's troops attempted to capture Culp's Hill. The Southern attack was slow and bloody. The hill was steep and had many large boulders that the soldiers had to climb over. It was hard for them to gain any ground. The rebels did very little damage, and the return fire from the Union troops was devastating.

By late in the day, the Southerners had a foothold near the bottom of the hill.

Ewell planned for an early attack at dawn the next day. He hoped to take the Northern enemy by surprise.

CHAPTER 5
Day Three: July 3, 1863

The Southern surprise attack never happened. Instead, at 4:30 a.m., Union soldiers opened fire on the Confederates on Culp's Hill. The Confederates fired back. The fighting was fierce. However, the rebels were stopped by a brigade of New York soldiers. They had dug in behind log fences that gave them good cover. Union sharpshooters were able to pick off Confederates as they tried to scramble up the steep hill.

Twice, the rebels tried to gain the hill. Both times they were thrown back. By midmorning, they had lost the ground gained the day before.

Besides the attack on Culp's Hill, Lee's plan for July 3 had two other parts. One part consisted of

a massive infantry attack of fifteen thousand men on the center of the long Union line. At the same time, General Jeb Stuart's cavalry would catch the enemy from behind.

Stuart was Lee's most trusted scout. Yet up until this point Stuart's men had not seen any action at Gettysburg.

When the Confederate Army went into

Pennsylvania at the end of June, Lee had given Stuart very clear orders. Stuart's cavalry was to scout for any Union troops that might be in Pennsylvania and report their numbers and movements to Lee. Stuart and his men had done this kind of scouting before. Lee was counting on them for accurate information now. But Stuart had not reported back. Why?

General Stuart

Almost as soon as Stuart started moving north, he met up with a Union wagon train. The wagons were filled with supplies that the rebels badly needed. Stuart's men easily captured the wagons, and Stuart decided to bring the valuable supplies to Lee. This was a bad decision.

Moving supplies slowed Stuart down so much

that Meade's Northern troops had moved into Pennsylvania without Lee knowing where they were. (It turned out they were only about twenty miles away.)

By the time Stuart learned that the two armies were at Gettysburg, the battle had started. Stuart finally abandoned the supply train and hurried to Lee's headquarters.

Lee, who was very fond of Stuart, greeted him coldly. If Lee had known that the Northern soldiers were so close by, he could have set up a surprise attack. Or he could have avoided them completely.

Now a cavalry attack on July 3 presented a chance for Stuart to redeem himself with a victory.

Meanwhile, General Longstreet was still trying to convince Lee to abandon the attack and move south. Once again, he argued that the Union position from Cemetery Hill along Cemetery Ridge to Little Round Top was too strong. Also, his soldiers were exhausted from the last two days of fighting. Fresh troops were needed.

"General, I have been a soldier all my life," Longstreet said. "It is my opinion that no fifteen thousand men ever arrayed for battle can take that position."

Jeb Stuart

James Ewell Brown (known as Jeb) Stuart was a Virginian like Robert E. Lee. He was born at Lauren Hill Farm on February 6, 1833. A graduate of West Point, Jeb Stuart was both a great soldier and a colorful character. He had a long flowing black beard and wore a scarlet-lined cape and bright yellow sash. His hat always sported an ostrich plume.

Like many families, Stuart's was divided by the Civil War. His wife, Flora, was the daughter of Union General Philip St. George Cooke. Yet Flora's brother, General John Rogers Cooke, fought for the Confederacy.

Stuart was known for his daring. On June 12, 1862, Stuart took a force of 1,200 troops and, in four days, circled around a gigantic gathering of more than 100,000 Union soldiers in Virginia. Stuart was able to report back to General Lee with important information about the enemy.

Stuart, however, let down his commander, Robert E. Lee, at Gettysburg. By the time Stuart arrived at the battle late on the second day, the battle was in full swing. On July 3, 1863, Stuart and his cavalry tried attacking the Union forces in a raid near Culp's Hill. But the attack was not successful.

After the Battle of Gettysburg was lost, Lee had Stuart and his men protect the Confederate Army as it retreated south.

Less than a year later, on May 11, 1864, Jeb Stuart was wounded at the Battle of Yellow Tavern, Virginia. He died the next day. He was only thirty-one years old.

By "that position," he meant the miles-long Union line. Fifteen thousand men were not enough to do the job.

Lee, however, still refused to listen. He was determined to stick with his plan. He still could defeat the enemy at Gettysburg. "We will attack," he told Longstreet.

CHAPTER 6
Day Three: Pickett's Charge

General Pickett

For the exhausted rebel troops, there was good news. General George Pickett, along with his 5,400 soldiers from Virginia, arrived late on the evening of July 2. They were the last to arrive at Gettysburg. Pickett's men had not fought at all yet. Lee combined them with parts of two other divisions. Still, the total number was only twelve thousand five hundred soldiers instead of the fifteen thousand that Lee had planned.

Lee had 160 cannons facing the Union lines. They would bombard and knock out the enemy cannons. Doing this would inflict heavy losses on the Northern soldiers. Then the rebels would charge a small grove of trees. Lee believed this was the weakest point of the Union line. If successful, this charge would split the Union line in half.

At one o'clock, all 160 Southern cannons fired at once. The noise was so loud that it was heard forty miles away in Harrisburg, Pennsylvania.

Union cannons answered back. Soon the entire battlefield was covered in thick white smoke from the cannons. Neither side could see the other.

Artillery crews (the soldiers working the cannons) could not aim properly. Most of the Confederate cannons were missing their targets completely. (The rebels did not know that.)

On the Union side, Brigadier General Henry Hunt was in command of the artillery. Hunt was experienced and smart. After the first hour of steady bombardment, he ordered his men to cease firing. Some cannons were moved back, out of sight. He wanted to fool the rebels into thinking that all the Union cannons had been knocked out.

The trick worked. When the fire from Union cannons stopped, the Confederates believed the enemy cannons were all destroyed. Still, the Southern bombardment went on for another hour until they were almost out of ammunition.

A Southern artillery officer sent a note to General George Pickett.

"The 18 [enemy] guns have been driven off.

For God's sake come quick or we cannot support you. Ammunition nearly out."

Pickett found Longstreet.

"General, shall I advance?" he asked.

Longstreet did not answer. He merely bowed his head.

Pickett took this as a yes. "I shall lead my division forward," Pickett told him.

The Confederate troops began their advance. The twelve thousand five hundred men had to cross three quarters of a mile of open fields in the heat.

The Union cannons waited for the rebels to get into close range. Union soldiers crouched behind a stone wall, ready with their rifles loaded.

The Union General Winfield Scott Hancock had only six thousand men left of the twelve thousand who had come with him to Gettysburg two days earlier. He watched the rebels advance. The flags of each regiment led the way.

Pickett's Charge

"Their lines were formed with a precision and steadiness," Hancock recalled later. He admired that. Onward the rebels marched.

On Seminary Ridge, Lee sat on his horse, Traveller. He could see his men getting closer and closer to the Union lines.

Suddenly the Union artillery opened fire. Within two or three minutes, hundreds of Confederates were killed* or wounded. Still,

Confederate officers urged their troops forward.

Then the Northern artillery began firing

canister shots from their cannons. Canister
shots were tin projectiles. Each one contained

hundreds of one-
and-a-half-inch
iron balls. The
canisters came apart
in the air and the iron balls
spread out like shotgun blasts.
Pickett's soldiers were blown to bits.

When what remained of the Confederate
infantry was only a hundred yards away, the
Union soldiers suddenly stood and fired a volley

straight into them. The whole front rank of Confederates was wiped out. Union riflemen targeted the Confederate officers. All but one were killed or wounded before they ever reached the enemy line.

General Hancock was riding behind the Union line observing the action. All of a sudden a bullet went through the top of his saddle and into his thigh. The wound was a severe one. Hancock was not expected to survive.

The "hooks" at each end of the long Union battle line swung out so Northern soldiers faced the flanks of the rebel troops. Now the Confederates were being shot at from three sides.

General Lewis Armistead was the only Confederate officer to reach the stone wall that marked the Union line. He was rushing forward with his sword out. Some of his men had just burst through the enemy line when Armistead was shot. Seconds later he was captured.

Armistead knew he was dying. Before the war, Armistead and Hancock had served together and become close friends. When the Southern states seceded, the two men found themselves on opposite sides of the war. Nevertheless, they agreed not to let that ruin their friendship. Now Armistead asked a Union officer to give his pocket watch, spurs, and other personal items to General Hancock.

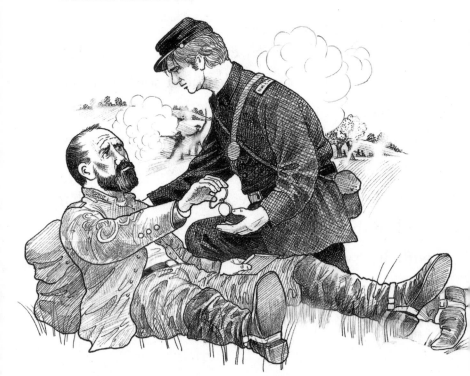

The officer told him that Hancock had been seriously wounded. It was uncertain whether he would survive, either.

"Tell General Hancock . . . I have done him and done you all an injury which I shall regret the longest day I live," Armistead said. He died two days later in a field hospital.

Hancock was luckier. He survived the war and later returned his friend's possessions to the Armistead family.

The spot where Armistead was shot is marked

with a stone monument. Besides honoring Armistead's bravery, the monument is at the "high-water mark" of the Confederate attack at

Gettysburg. Pickett's Charge, as it is called, was the Confederacy's last chance to defeat the Union and win the war. And it was a disaster. The rebels were retreating as quickly as they could. Many were wounded and had to be helped off the battlefield. Many more were too weak to move.

Hundreds of bodies littered the battleground.

As General Pickett and his retreating soldiers drew closer to their own line, they saw a familiar gray-bearded figure sitting on his gray horse. It was General Lee. He told Pickett to prepare his troops for a counterattack.

General Pickett had just watched Union cannons mow down nearly all his men. "General," Pickett told Lee, "I have no division."

Some stories say that Lee went up to survivors of the charge and said, "All this has been my fault." But Lee never mentions this in books he wrote about the Civil War.

At the end of the day, each army was holding almost the same position it had when the sun had risen that morning. And nearly ten thousand more soldiers were dead. The day had been very costly for the Confederates. Their losses numbered over seven thousand men. By comparison, the Union Army had lost around three thousand men.

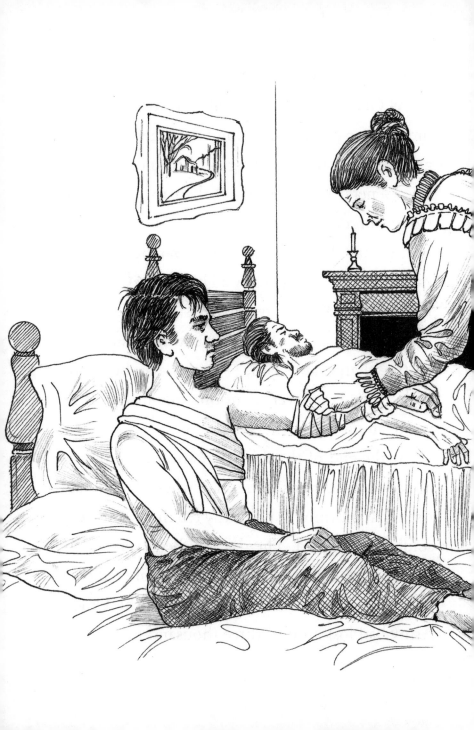

In Gettysburg, any place with a roof and room for wounded men became a temporary hospital. The townspeople helped in any way they could. Union doctors worked around the clock to save lives. Wounded Union and Confederate soldiers lay together.

Lee and Meade spent the evening meeting with their officers going over supplies and figuring out how many troops were still able to fight. Each commander tried to guess his opponent's next move.

Lee was expecting Meade to counterattack. Lee's plan for a decisive victory in Gettysburg had not worked. Now Lee was going to do what General Longstreet had advised all along. The Southern army—what was left of it—would head back south.

General Meade of the North knew that General Lee was a tough fighter who did not like to give up. But still Meade expected that Lee and his men would retreat. So Meade did not plan for a counterattack the next day.

CHAPTER 7
The Day After: July 4, 1863

On Independence Day, both armies totaled up "the butcher's bill." That is military slang for the number of men killed, wounded, and missing.

The totals for the three-day battle were twenty-three thousand Union Army soldiers killed, wounded, or missing and twenty-seven thousand killed, wounded, or missing on the Southern side.

General Lee informed his officers that they would begin the retreat to Virginia that afternoon. He ordered every available wagon be used to carry the wounded.

When the wagon train got underway, it was seventeen miles long. Heavy rain was coming down. The dirt roads quickly turned into mud. The mud slowed down the Confederate wagons.

**The Confederate wagon train,
seventeen miles long**

Abraham Lincoln, Commander in Chief

Today, Abraham Lincoln is regarded as one of the greatest presidents of the United States. But his election in 1860 split the country and started a war. As president, Lincoln was also commander in chief of the army and navy. In the first two years of the war, the North won only one out of five major battles. Lincoln blamed his top generals. They weren't aggressive enough. They had "the slows."

Lee had Stuart camp his men across from Cemetery Ridge. This helped screen the retreating Confederates from view.

Even so, Meade knew Lee's army was in retreat. He had received early reports that the rebels were moving out. An aggressive general would have pursued the enemy. But Meade was cautious. Too cautious. He chose to wait another day while his troops rested and were resupplied. Also, he had no desire to fight the Confederate rear guard in the narrow passes of South Mountain.

When Lincoln heard that Meade was not in hot pursuit of Lee and his battered army, he was furious. Meade had made some good decisions during the three-day battle. Why couldn't he finish off the Southerners now? Instead, Lee and his troops had been allowed to escape.

And the Civil War went on for almost two more bloody years.

Lincoln's Top Generals

Lincoln's first top general was George B. McClellan. Then came General Joseph "Fighting Joe" Hooker. After that was George G. Meade, who was in command at Gettysburg. Lincoln wanted generals like Robert E. Lee, who were tough and determined to win. He finally found such leaders in General Ulysses S. Grant (who later became the eighteenth president), General William Tecumseh Sherman, and General Philip H. Sheridan. Their aggressive tactics won the war for the North, bringing the Union back together.

George B. McClellan

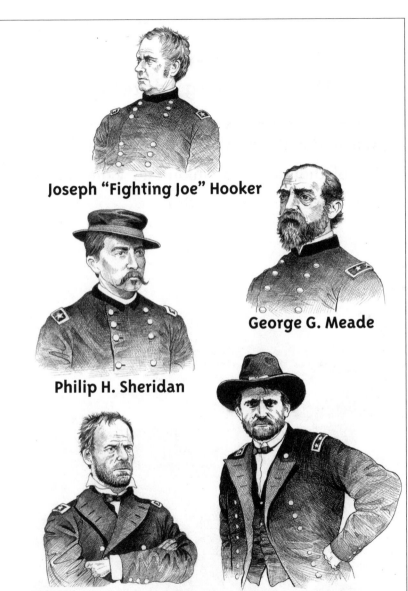

Joseph "Fighting Joe" Hooker

George G. Meade

Philip H. Sheridan

William Tecumseh Sherman   Ulysses S. Grant

CHAPTER 8
The Gettysburg Address

When the Battle of Gettysburg ended, the bodies of thousands of Union and Confederate soldiers lay across the battlefield.

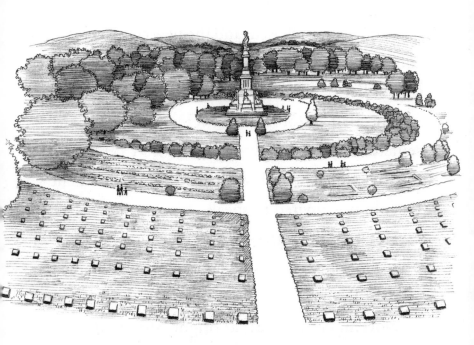

They had to be buried quickly. Many were placed in shallow graves very close to where they died.

Within a few weeks, some important citizens and politicians in Pennsylvania decided to establish a special cemetery at Gettysburg. It was called the Soldiers' National Cemetery at Gettysburg. (Confederate soldiers remained in their original battlefield graves until after the Civil War.)

Land was purchased, and the new cemetery was laid out in two half circles around a monument to the soldiers.

The first 1,258 bodies were reburied in the cemetery by mid-November 1863. A ceremony was scheduled for November 19, and President Lincoln was invited to speak.

He was not the main speaker, however. That honor went to a famous orator named Edward Everett.

November 19 was a bright sunny day in Gettysburg. Before a crowd of fifteen to twenty thousand people, Edward Everett went first, speaking from a small stage. He spoke for two hours. He said that the Battle of Gettysburg would take its place alongside the most famous battles in the history of the world. Then it was the president's turn.

Abraham Lincoln had written a very short speech, so short that the story was that he wrote

Edward Everett speaking

it quickly on the train to Gettysburg. But that is not true. Although the speech is only 271 words long, it is one of the most beautiful and moving speeches in all of American history. Today it is known as the Gettysburg Address.

Abraham Lincoln did not talk about the battle, but about the young men who had died fighting. Lincoln could see more than a thousand new headstones planted in the ground. Lincoln said that the young soldiers had not died "in vain"—for nothing. They had fought to keep the country together as George Washington and the

Founding Fathers meant it to be. Lincoln wanted the Southern states to know they would be welcomed back into the Union, once the North won and peace returned.

The crowd did not seem to think it was a great speech; Lincoln said that it "fell like a wet blanket." However, Edward Everett wrote the president the next day. "I should be glad, if I could flatter myself that I came as near to the central idea of the occasion, in two hours, as you did in two minutes."

Gettysburg Today

Today the Gettysburg National Cemetery holds the bodies of over 3,500 soldiers who died at Gettysburg, including young Charlie Spiesberger.

More than one million people visit Gettysburg every year. That is far more than the number of visitors to any other Civil War battleground. The cemetery and battlegrounds are open all year. At certain times of the year there are dramatic reenactments of the battle with actors playing Union and Confederate soldiers. There is also a museum with exhibits that explain what happened over those three important days.

The Gettysburg Address

Four score and seven years ago our fathers brought forth, on this continent, a new nation, conceived in Liberty, and dedicated to the proposition that all men are created equal.

Now we are engaged in a great civil war, testing whether that nation, or any nation so conceived and so dedicated, can long endure. We are met on a great battle-field of that war. We have come to dedicate a portion of that field, as a final resting place for those who here gave their lives, that this nation might live. It is altogether fitting and proper that we should do this.

But in a larger sense, we cannot dedicate— we cannot consecrate—we cannot hallow this ground. The brave men, living and dead, who struggled here, have consecrated it far above our poor power to add or subtract. The world will little note, nor long remember what we say here, but it can never forget what they did here. It is for us the living, rather, to be dedicated here to the unfinished work which they who fought here have thus far so nobly advanced. It is rather for us the living to be dedicated to the great task remaining before us that from these honored dead we take increased devotion to that cause for which they here gave the last full measure of devotion—that we here highly resolve that these dead shall not have died in vain—that this nation, under God, shall have a new birth of freedom—and that government of the people, by the people, for the people, shall not perish from the earth.

A Soldier's Letter Home

140th Reg. N.Y. Vols

Camp near Falmouth Va.

Saturday Feb. 20/63

Dear Parents - Brothers & Sisters

I [received] letter [ck] 19 last evening in which you told me of the [second] box which had sent by mail. I am glad you have sent the second box off [there] is some things in it I want to use. I have seen nothing yet of either [boxes]. I told you in my last letter that I was sick. I am now well again [and] able do duty. I had king of [Fever & Ague] We are to have a Brigade [Bakery]. They are at work to-day building it. I hope it will soon be finished and put in use. We have now to make up our flour rations in some [shape] to eat ourselves and [is] not a very pleasant [job]. The weather to-day is beautiful the sun [coming] out warm and pleasant and the boys are out warming themselves. We send out [details] every day if the weather will allow to work on a fortification which they are throwing up on the Rail-Road about two miles from us. I have not yet been out but expect to have to take my turn before many days. One thing, the boys do not [hurt] themselves to work I can assure [you]. They know . . .

and [ ] for a move of the Grand Army in Rochester. We are not in any hurry here about moving on to Richmond. I do not think those who are so fast to [urge us in] would be either if they were here with us. The soldiers are not so eager to fight as [many] suppose because they do not see that [it will end] the war. The Old 13th will soon leave us their

[very little respect for the .... Reg]

You had better use the [Greenbacks] I left to fix up the [House]. They are getting [most too plenty]. You will then have a [sure] thing of getting the [worth] of them. [Still] you can do as you think best. If you do use keep some for yourselves to live on or you can use it on the Barn. Just as you [think]

Best from your son

With love to all.

Charlie

Courtesy of Jim O'Connor

Charles Spiesberger, Union private from Company D of the 140th New York Volunteer Infantry, who died in the Battle of Gettysburg, and the uncle of the author's grandfather

Timeline of the Battle of Gettysburg

1860 — Abraham Lincoln is elected president

— South Carolina secedes from the Union

1861 — Ten more Southern states secede from the Union

— Civil War begins

1863 — Emancipation Proclamation, freeing slaves in the rebel states, takes effect on January 1

— Battle of Gettysburg begins on July 1

— Confederate troops leave Gettysburg on July 4

— Lincoln delivers the Gettysburg Address on November 19

1865 — Lee surrenders at Appomattox Courthouse in Virginia

— Lincoln is assassinated in Washington, DC

— Reconstruction begins under President Andrew Johnson

— The Thirteenth Amendment is passed, abolishing slavery

1870 — General Lee dies

1872 — General Meade dies

1895 — Congress establishes the Gettysburg National Military Park

Timeline of the World

Three-Fifths Compromise (the North and the South agree that three-fifths of a state's slave population will count for representation and tax purposes) is reached	1787
Cotton gin is invented, increasing demand for slaves in the South	1793
Slave Nat Turner's rebellion takes place in Virginia, where more than fifty white inhabitants are killed before Turner's capture	1831
Most African Americans in the North are free by this time	1840
Second Opium War concludes in China	1860
First permanent transatlantic telegraph cable is successfully laid	1866
Alfred Nobel receives patent for dynamite	1867
The Alaskan territory is purchased from Russia	
First Transcontinental Railroad is completed in the United States	1869
Suez Canal in Egypt opens	
Alexander Graham Bell invents the telephone	1876
Tuskegee Institute, a historically black university, is founded	1881

Bibliography

Hansen, Harry. *The Civil War: A History*. New York: New American Library, 2002.

LaFantasie, Glenn W. *Twilight at Little Round Top: July 2, 1863—The Tide Turns at Gettysburg*. Hoboken, NJ: John Wiley & Sons, 2005.

Masur, Louis P. *The Civil War: A Concise History*. New York: Oxford University Press, 2011.

McPherson, James M. *Hallowed Ground: A Walk at Gettysburg*. New York: Crown Publishers, 2003.

Stanchak, John. *Civil War*. New York: DK Publishing, 2011.

Symonds, Craig L. *American Heritage History of the Battle of Gettysburg*. New York: HarperCollins, 2001.

Wheeler, Richard. *Gettysburg 1863: Campaign of Endless Echoes*. New York: Plume, 1999.